Hooray! It's Passover!

Hooray! It's Passover!

by Leslie Kimmelman
illustrated by John Himmelman

SCHOLASTIC INC.
New York Toronto London Auckland Sydney
Mexico City New Delhi Hong Kong

ISBN 0-439-18710-9

Text copyright © 1996 by Leslie A. Kimmelman.
Illustrations copyright © 1996 by John Himmelman. All rights reserved.
Published by Scholastic Inc., 555 Broadway, New York, NY 10012,
by arrangement with HarperTrophy, a division of HarperCollins
Children's Books, a division of HarperCollins Publishers.
SCHOLASTIC and associated logos are trademarks
and/or registered trademarks of Scholastic Inc.

12 11 10 9 8 7 6 5 4 3   1 2 3 4 5/0

Printed in the U.S.A.   09

First Scholastic printing, April 2000

This is for Gregory—I love you.

—L.K.

For my family.

—J.H.

It's Passover! My relatives come from far and near to share our Seder dinner.

First we will hear of the days when Jews were slaves

in the land of Egypt. We will taste the special

Passover foods. Crunchy matzah is my favorite.

I pass out the Haggadot.

My mother lights the holiday candles.

My father blesses the wine. We leave a glass of wine and an empty chair for Elijah.

We all dip parsley in salt water.

My little brother asks the special Passover questions. "Why is this night different from all other nights?" he begins.

My grampa tells the story of the cruel Pharaoh, and
of brave Moses, who led the Jews to freedom.

My cousins sing "Dayenu," a happy Passover song.

We wash our hands right at the table.

Then my father says the prayer over the matzah.

My uncles eat bitter herbs on their matzah.

My aunts like sweet haroset better.

It's time for dinner. My grandmothers serve chicken soup and matzah balls.

Our cats sniff the gefilte fish.

After dinner the children hunt for the afikomen—a piece of matzah that has been wrapped in a napkin and hidden. I wonder where it will be.

Could it be under the sofa? On top of the piano?

Whoever finds it will get a special treat.

I found it! Hooray!

Happy, happy Passover!

THE STORY OF PASSOVER

Every spring, for eight days, Jewish people all over the world celebrate Passover. On the first two nights, family and friends gather for a holiday dinner called a *Seder*. They read from Passover prayer books, *Haggadot*, praying and singing and telling the story of when Jews were slaves in the land of Egypt.

Over three thousand years ago, a cruel Pharaoh ruled over Egypt. He made all Jews slaves and ordered that every firstborn Jewish boy be killed. One mother saved her baby by floating him down the river in a basket. The basket was found by the Pharaoh's daughter, who named the boy Moses and raised him as an Egyptian prince.

When Moses grew up, he saw how harshly the Jews were treated. Then God spoke to him, saying, "With my help, you will lead the Jewish people to freedom. You must go to the Pharaoh and say, *'Let my people go!'*" Moses did this, but the Pharaoh would not listen. So God punished the Egyptians with ten plagues. The last was the worst. God caused the oldest child of every Egyptian family to die but passed over the houses where Jewish families lived. When his own son died, the Pharaoh finally freed the slaves. The Jews followed Moses out of Egypt quickly, for they knew the Pharaoh could change his mind. They did not even wait for their bread to rise.

That is why crunchy, flat bread called *matzah* is eaten during Passover. Many Seder foods celebrate the escape from Egypt. Parsley stands for springtime, and salt water for the tears cried by the slaves. Bitter herbs are a reminder of the bitterness of slavery, and haroset, a mixture of nuts, apples, and wine, stands for the mortar used to build the Pharaoh's cities. Looking for the *afikomen* ("dessert" in Greek) is another tradition. Finally, at the Seder's end, a door is opened for the prophet Elijah, who Jews believe will come to announce a time of peace and happiness in the world. There is always an extra cup of wine for Elijah at the table.

Most of all, the Seder reminds us of the importance of freedom. The Jews hope that someday everyone in the world will be free.